SELECT SERIES

Beans & Rice

by JEAN PARÉ

Christmas 2002.

Love Mom xo

COOKBOOKS

Beans & Rice

First printing May 1997
Canadian Cataloguing in Publication Data
Paré, Jean
        Beans & rice

Includes index.
Published also in French under title: Haricots et riz.
ISBN 1-896891-06-3

    1. Cookery (Beans). 2. Cookery (Rice). I. Title.
II. Title: Beans and rice.

TX803.B4P37 1997   641.6'565   C97-900064-5

Published simultaneously in
Canada and the United States of America by
The Recipe Factory Inc.
in conjunction with
Company's Coming Publishing Limited
2311 - 96 Street
Edmonton, Alberta, Canada T6N 1G3
Tel: 403 • 450-6223
Fax: 403 • 450-1857

COOKBOOKS®

Beans & Rice was created thanks to the dedicated efforts of the people and organizations listed below.

COMPANY'S COMING PUBLISHING LIMITED

Author	Jean Paré
President	Grant Lovig
Production Manager	Kathy Knowles
Production Coordinator	Derrick Sorochan
Design	Nora Cserny
Typesetting	Marlene Crosbie
	Debbie Dixon

THE RECIPE FACTORY INC.

Managing Editor	Nora Prokop
Test Kitchen Supervisor	Lynda Elsenheimer
Assistant Editor	Stephanie With
Photographer	Stephe Tate Photo
Food Stylist	Stephanie With
Prop Stylist	Gabriele McEleney

Our special thanks to the following businesses for providing extensive props for photography.

Chintz & Company
Creations By Design
Enchanted Kitchen
La Cache
Le Gnome
Stokes
The Bay Housewares Dept.

Color separations, printing, and binding by Friesens, Altona, Manitoba, Canada
Printed in Canada

FRONT COVER
Clockwise from top right:
Jambalaya, page 73
Overnight Bean Salad, page 31
Vegetarian Bean Soup, page 38

Table of Contents

The Jean Paré Story

Jean Paré grew up understanding that the combination of family, friends and home cooking is the essence of a good life. From her mother she learned to appreciate good cooking, while her father praised even her earliest attempts. When she left home she took with her many acquired family recipes, her love of cooking and her intriguing desire to read recipe books like novels!

In 1963, when her four children had all reached school age, Jean volunteered to cater to the 50th anniversary of the Vermilion School of Agriculture, now Lakeland College. Working out of her home, Jean prepared a dinner for over 1000 people which launched a flourishing catering operation that continued for over eighteen years. During that time she was provided with countless opportunities to test new ideas with immediate feedback—resulting in empty plates and contented customers! Whether preparing cocktail sandwiches for a house party or serving a hot meal for 1500 people, Jean Paré earned a reputation for good food, courteous service and reasonable prices.

"Why don't you write a cookbook?" Time and again, as requests for her recipes mounted, Jean was asked that question. Jean's response was to team up with her son, Grant Lovig, in the fall of 1980 to form Company's Coming Publishing Limited. April 14, 1981, marked the debut of "150 DELICIOUS SQUARES", the first Company's Coming cookbook in what soon would become Canada's most popular cookbook series. By 1995, sales had surpassed ten million cookbooks.

Jean Paré's operation has grown from the early days of working out of a spare bedroom in her home to operating a large and fully equipped test kitchen in Vermilion, Alberta, near the home she and her husband Larry built. Full-time staff has grown steadily to include marketing personnel located in major cities across Canada plus selected U.S. markets. Home Office is located in Edmonton, Alberta where distribution, accounting and administration functions are headquartered in the company's own 20,000 square foot facility. Growth continues with the recent addition of the Recipe Factory, a 2700 square foot test kitchen and photography studio located in Edmonton.

Company's Coming cookbooks are now distributed throughout Canada and the United States plus numerous overseas markets, all under the guidance of Jean's daughter, Gail Lovig. The series is published in English and French, plus a Spanish language edition is available in Mexico. Soon the familiar and trusted Company's Coming style of recipes will be available in a variety of formats in addition to the bestselling soft cover series.

Jean Paré's approach to cooking has always called for quick and easy recipes using everyday ingredients. She continues to gain new supporters by adhering to what she calls "the golden rule of cooking": never share a recipe you wouldn't use yourself. It's an approach that works—*ten million times over!*

Foreword

Beans and rice have long been popular ingredients in international cuisine. It's due in part to today's health-conscious lifestyle that they now enjoy a renewed popularity in everyday food preparation. As more varieties of beans and rice become available to us through our local grocer, so do we discover the need for a book such as this!

In the first section you will find recipes that feature both the garden-variety bean (green beans, yellow wax beans) and the dried bean variety such as kidney beans, black beans, and lentils. It is this second variety that has become such a common ingredient in vegetarian-style cooking. They can provide a delicious and satisfying meal while helping you reduce fat and cholesterol intake. Popularity of cooking with beans as a main ingredient has prodded many grocery stores to begin stocking more varieties on their shelves, which means that we now have a good selection of both dried beans and their canned counterparts to choose from. A chart is shown on page 6 that identifies the many varieties of beans commonly used and their characteristics.

Dried beans need to be cooked before using in a recipe, however it isn't necessary to soak them beforehand. You should first select and pick through your beans to remove any debris, then add them to a pot of rapidly boiling, salted water. Cover, reduce heat and cook until tender.

Refer to the chart on page 6 for cooking times. Your beans are now ready to be used. If time is of the essence, canned beans are a very convenient and equally successful alternative ingredient.

Rice, like beans, is a simple and popular ingredient that has a long history of use in international cuisine. It demonstrates a surprising versatility as part of a salad, side dish, main course, soup, dessert and even pizza crust! High in carbohydrates and low in fat, rice makes any meal both delicious and satisfying. There is no secret to successfully cooking rice—simply follow recipe directions and measure out your ingredients carefully. Rice can be made ahead of time and frozen for up to six months—ready to be used by simply warming slowly on your stove or in the microwave oven. Page 43 of this book identifies some of the more common varieties of rice that are readily available.

Beans & Rice is an excellent source of delicious recipes for you to consider when planning your next meal. Look to a satisfying Three Bean Bake, page 8, when friends drop in, or Wild Rice And Seafood Salad, page 58, when you need a dish for the buffet table. Jambalaya, page 73, is certain to bring a little of that southern Louisiana charm into your kitchen. With recipes for every occasion at your fingertips, you are more than ready to serve up something spectacular!

Glossary of Beans

BEAN	COLOR	SIZE	SHAPE	DRIED	CANNED	COOKING TIME FOR DRIED
Black beans	Black	Medium	Oval	✔	✔	1-1½ hours
Black-eyed beans (Black-eyed peas)	Cream with black "eye"	Medium	Round	✔	✔	¾-1 hour
Chick peas (Garbanzo beans)	Cream	Medium-large	Acorn	✔	✔	1-2 hours
Fava beans (Broad beans)	Red-brown or green	Large or small	Broad	✔	✔	2 hours
Great northern beans (Haricot beans)	White	Medium-large	Oval	✔	✔	1-1½ hours
Kidney beans (Mexican beans)	Dark and light red	Large	Kidney-shaped	✔	✔	1-1½ hours
Lentils	Varied	Small	Narrow oval	✔	✔	¾ hour
Lima beans • Small (Butter beans Calico beans)	Pale white	Small	Thumbnail	✔	✔	1 hour
• Large	Cream	Large	Wide	✔	✔	1-1½ hours
Navy beans (White pea)	White	Small	Oval	✔	✔	1-1½ hours
Pinto beans	Pinkish brown mottled	Medium	Oval	✔	✔	1 hour
Soybeans (soya beans)	Tan or yellow	Large	Round	Soy sauce, soy milk, soybean oil, tofu		
Split peas (Field peas)	Green or yellow	Small	Round-split in ½	✔	✗	1¼-1½ hours

When beans are an ingredient in your casserole, you have a nutritious and satisfying meal that is both high in protein and fiber. These recipes are easy to prepare and convenient for serving as either a side dish or main course. You will also discover these delicious casseroles are ideal as part of a buffet because they go well with practically any other dish!

BAKED BEANS AND PINEAPPLE

Everyday beans dressed up for company.

Cooking oil	1 tbsp.	15 mL
Chopped onion	1 cup	250 mL
Canned deep browned beans in tomato sauce	19 oz.	540 mL
Canned red kidney beans, with liquid	14 oz.	398 mL
Canned crushed pineapple, with juice	1 cup	250 mL
Ketchup	1/3 cup	75 mL
Prepared mustard	1 tsp.	5 mL
Brown sugar, packed	1/2 cup	125 mL
Simulated bacon bits	1 tbsp.	15 mL
Worcestershire sauce	1/4 tsp.	1 mL
Salt	1/4 tsp.	1 mL
Pepper	1/8 tsp.	0.5 mL

Heat cooking oil in frying pan. Add onion and sauté slowly until soft. Put in 2 quart (2 L) casserole.

Add remaining ingredients in order given. Stir to mix. Bake, uncovered, in 350°F (175°C) oven for 1 1/2 hours until bubbly. Stir once or twice during baking. Serves 6 to 8.

Pictured on page 11.

THREE BEAN BAKE

A sweet and sour combination. A topping of buttered crumbs may be added to fancy it up or serve as is.

Bacon slices	8	8
Thinly sliced onion	2 cups	500 mL
Brown sugar, packed	½ cup	125 mL
Cider vinegar	¼ cup	60 mL
Salt	½ tsp.	2 mL
Pepper	⅛ tsp.	0.5 mL
Dry mustard powder	½ tsp.	2 mL
Canned baked beans in tomato sauce	14 oz.	398 mL
Canned kidney beans, with liquid	14 oz.	398 mL
Canned lima beans, drained	14 oz.	398 mL

Fry bacon until crisp. Remove from frying pan. Crumble. Drain fat from frying pan.

Add onion to frying pan.

Add sugar, vinegar, salt, pepper and mustard. Stir. Cover and cook slowly for 20 minutes.

Mix all beans with onion mixture and bacon and put into ungreased 2 quart (2 L) casserole. Bake, uncovered, in 350°F (175°C) oven for about 30 minutes. Serves 8.

Pictured below.

BAKED BEANS

Made from scratch, these will bring back memories to many. No need to presoak beans but if you prefer to do so, you save about twenty minutes baking time. These may be completely cooked on top of the stove.

Navy beans	2¼ cups	550 mL
Water	6 cups	1.5 L
Mild molasses	½ cup	125 mL
Chopped onion	½ cup	125 mL
Brown sugar, packed	½ cup	125 mL
White vinegar	2 tbsp.	30 mL
Bacon slices, cut up	4	4
Salt	1 tsp.	5 mL
Garlic powder	⅛ tsp.	0.5 mL
Ketchup	¼ cup	60 mL
Ketchup	2 tbsp.	30 mL
Bacon slices, cut up and half-cooked	2	2

Place beans and water in large saucepan. Bring to a boil. Cover. Simmer about 50 minutes until beans can be bitten into easily.

Add next 8 ingredients. Stir to mix. Transfer to bean pot. If there isn't room for all the liquid, save it to add as beans cook. Bake, covered, in 300°F (150°C) oven for 2½ hours.

Spread second amount of ketchup over top. Put second amount of bacon over ketchup. Continue to bake, uncovered, for ½ hour or until cooked. Serves 8.

PARÉ *pointer*

When you are finally old enough to know all the answers, nobody asks you any questions.

Baked Beans and Pineapple, page 7

TOMATO BEAN DISH

The red and green colors make this particularly festive. Best made the day of serving.

Frozen green beans, cooked and drained	6 cups	1.5 L
Medium tomatoes, chopped	6	6
Grated medium or sharp Cheddar cheese	2 cups	500 mL
TOPPING		
Large eggs	4	4
Milk	1 cup	250 mL
Biscuit mix	1 cup	250 mL
Salt	1 tsp.	5 mL
Cayenne pepper	½ tsp.	2 mL
Dried sweet basil	1 tsp.	5 mL

Spread green beans in layer in ungreased 9 x 13 inch (22 x 33 cm) pan. Layer tomatoes over top. Sprinkle with cheese.

Topping: Beat eggs in large bowl. Add milk, biscuit mix, salt, cayenne and basil. Beat. Pour over cheese. Bake, uncovered, in 350°F (175°C) oven for about 50 minutes until browned and heated through. Serves 10 to 12.

Pictured below.

P A R É
pointer

Is it a coincidence

that the word

improvement begins

with "I"?

GREEN BEAN CASSEROLE

A different twist with a winning flavor.

Butter or hard margarine	3 tbsp.	50 mL
Chopped onion	1 cup	250 mL
All-purpose flour	¼ cup	60 mL
Salt	1 tsp.	5 mL
Pepper	½ tsp.	2 mL
Milk	1½ cups	375 mL
Soy sauce	2 tsp.	10 mL
Grated medium Cheddar cheese	3 cups	750 mL
Canned French-style green beans, drained	2 × 14 oz.	2 × 398 mL
Canned mushroom pieces, drained	10 oz.	284 mL
Toasted sliced almonds	½ cup	125 mL

Melt butter in frying pan. Add onion. Sauté until soft.

Mix in flour, salt and pepper. Stir in milk and soy sauce. Heat and stir until mixture boils and thickens.

Stir in cheese.

Place beans and mushrooms in greased 3 quart (3 L) casserole. Add onion mixture. Stir lightly from bottom to combine.

Sprinkle with almonds. Bake, uncovered, in 350°F (175°C) oven for about 30 minutes until bubbly hot. Serves 8.

PARÉ
pointer

Parents want their

children to reach

automatic drive

without becoming

shiftless.

CHOW MEIN GREEN BEANS

It takes but a few ingredients to make this.

Condensed cream of chicken soup (or cream of celery)	10 oz.	284 mL
Canned green beans, any style, drained	2 × 14 oz.	2 × 398 mL
Canned chow mein noodles	4 oz.	113 g
Grated Cheddar cheese	1½ cups	375 mL

Mix soup and beans together. Turn into greased 2 quart (2 L) casserole.

Cover with noodles. Sprinkle cheese over all. Cover and bake in 350°F (175°C) oven for 20 minutes. Remove cover and continue to bake for 10 to 15 minutes until cheese melts and toasts. Serves 6 to 8.

CURRY BEAN BAKE

Dark with a mild curry flavor. Increase amount of curry to suit taste. Easy to double recipe.

Canned kidney beans, with liquid, ground or mashed	14 oz.	398 mL
Ground walnuts (or other nuts)	1 cup	250 mL
Large eggs, beaten	3	3
Ketchup	3 tbsp.	50 mL
Curry powder	½ tsp.	2 mL
Ground sage	½ tsp.	2 mL
Salt	1 tsp.	5 mL
Celery salt	½ tsp.	2 mL
Bulgur	⅓ cup	75 mL

Combine all 9 ingredients in bowl. Mix well. Turn into greased 1 quart (1 L) casserole. Bake, uncovered, in 350°F (175°C) oven for 45 to 50 minutes until set. Serves 6.

TIP

Store cooked beans, covered, in the refrigerator up to 3 days or freeze up to 8 months.

GREEN BEAN CHESTNUT BAKE

Crunchy with a nice bit of flavor from the fried onion rings. A snap to make.

Condensed cream of mushroom soup	**10 oz.**	**284 mL**
Canned sliced water chestnuts	**5 oz.**	**142 g**
Process cheese slices, broken up (or 1 cup, 250 mL grated Cheddar cheese)	**4 × 1 oz.**	**4 × 28 g**
Hot pepper sauce	**¼ tsp.**	**1 mL**
Canned French-style green beans, drained	**2 × 14 oz.**	**2 × 398 mL**
Canned French fried onion rings	**3 oz.**	**85 g**

Heat first 4 ingredients in saucepan.

Stir in beans. Turn into greased 2 quart (2 L) casserole. Bake, uncovered, in 350°F (175°C) oven for 20 to 30 minutes until hot.

Cover with onion rings. Bake an additional 5 minutes. This may be poured directly from saucepan into serving bowl then covered with onions. Onions may be used at room temperature right from can or heated in oven first. Serves 6 to 8.

PARÉ
pointer

There was soup on

the menu until the

waiter wiped it off.

Named for the spice that dominates the flavors, chili dishes are popular, quick and simple to prepare. The secret to good chili is to simmer it for at least one hour, stirring often. You will find that the flavor of your chili improves when served the next day. These recipes are easily doubled and freeze well. Thaw, then reheat, stirring often.

CHICKEN CHILI

This is a medium-flavored chili. Add more chili powder to taste if you like.

Cooking oil	2 tbsp.	30 mL
Chopped onion	2 cups	500 mL
Lean ground raw chicken	2 lbs.	900 g
All-purpose flour	2 tbsp.	30 mL
Canned tomatoes, with juice, broken up	14 oz.	398 mL
Canned kidney beans, with liquid	2 x 14 oz.	2 x 398 mL
Chili powder	1 tbsp.	15 mL
Beef bouillon powder	1 tbsp.	15 mL
Salt	1 tsp.	5 mL
Pepper	1/4 tsp.	1 mL
Whole oregano	1/4 tsp.	1 mL
Granulated sugar	1/2 tsp.	2 mL
Worcestershire sauce	1/2 tsp.	2 mL

Heat cooking oil in frying pan. Add onion and ground chicken. Scramble-fry until browned.

Mix in flour. Stir in tomatoes until mixture boils.

Put next 8 ingredients into Dutch oven. Add chicken mixture. Stir. Bring to a boil. Simmer for 30 minutes, stirring often. Makes 7²/₃ cups (1.9 L).

CHILI

Colorful, chunky and very good and satisfying. Makes a family size or small party size quantity.

Cooking oil	2 tbsp.	30 mL
Chopped onion	3 cups	750 mL
Green pepper, chopped	1	1
Red pepper, chopped	1	1
Canned kidney beans, drained	2 x 14 oz.	2 x 398 mL
Canned pinto beans, drained	14 oz.	398 mL
Medium eggplant, peeled and diced	1	1
Canned stewed tomatoes	14 oz.	398 mL
Condensed tomato soup	10 oz.	284 mL
Cider vinegar	1 tbsp.	15 mL
Brown sugar, packed	¼ cup	60 mL
Chili powder	2 tbsp.	30 mL
Canned sliced mushrooms, drained	10 oz.	284 mL
Garlic powder	½ tsp.	2 mL
Salt	1 tsp.	5 mL
Pepper	¼ tsp.	1 mL

Heat cooking oil in frying pan. Add onion and peppers. Sauté until onion is soft. This may need to be done in two batches. Turn into large saucepan or Dutch oven.

Add remaining ingredients. Heat, stirring often until mixture starts to boil. Boil slowly, uncovered, for 5 to 10 minutes, stirring occasionally. Makes 10¼ cups (2.6 L), enough for 5 servings.

Pictured on this page.

CHILI CON CARNE

This oven chili may also be simmered on top of the stove. Extra chili powder may be added if desired.

Lean ground beef	2 lbs.	900 g
All-purpose flour	2 tbsp.	30 mL
Water	2 cups	500 mL
Tomato paste	5½ oz.	156 mL
Chopped onion	3 cups	750 mL
Canned kidney beans, with liquid	2 × 14 oz.	2 × 398 mL
Chili powder	1 tbsp.	15 mL
Celery seed	¼ tsp.	1 mL
Ground cumin	1 tsp.	5 mL
Pepper	¼ tsp.	1 mL
Garlic powder	¼ tsp.	1 mL
Liquid sweetener	1 tsp.	5 mL

Spray frying pan with no-stick cooking spray. Add ground beef. Scramble-fry until browned.

Mix in flour. Add water and tomato paste. Stir until mixture boils and thickens.

Add remaining ingredients. Stir. Turn into ungreased 3 quart (3 L) casserole. Cover. Bake in 350°F (175°C) oven for about 1 hour until flavors are blended. Makes 9¼ cups (2.3 L).

PARÉ
pointer

Does anyone know

when the first white

Dalmatian was

spotted?

Bean dips are very popular and quick to make when you use canned beans. Serve them with crackers or vegetables, wedges of pita bread or any other bread. If your dip is too thick for dipping, just serve it with a cocktail knife and you have a tasty spread!

BLACK BEAN DIP

A darkish dip with cheese sprinkled over top. Cider vinegar gives it a good tang.

Canned black beans, drained	19 oz.	540 mL
Cider vinegar	2 tsp.	10 mL
Salt	1/2 tsp.	2 mL
Pepper	1/8 tsp.	0.5 mL
Garlic powder	1/4 tsp.	1 mL
Onion powder	1/4 tsp.	1 mL
Hot pepper sauce (optional)	1/4-1/2 tsp.	1-2 mL
TOPPING		
Grated medium Cheddar cheese	1/4 cup	60 mL
Ground walnuts	1 tbsp.	15 mL
Tortilla chips, corn chips or raw vegetables		

Mash beans well with fork on plate. Turn into bowl.

Add next 6 ingredients. Stir. Transfer to serving dish.

Topping: Sprinkle cheese and walnuts over top. Chill until needed.

Serve with tortilla chips, corn chips or raw vegetables. Makes 1 1/3 cups (325 mL).

HUMMUS

Light in color, tasty and nutty in flavor. HOOM-uhs has a bit of a lemony tang.

Canned chick peas (garbanzo beans), drained and liquid reserved	**19 oz.**	**540 mL**
Lemon juice, fresh or bottled	**¼ cup**	**60 mL**
Tahini (sesame spread), see below	**⅓ cup**	**75 mL**
Garlic powder	**½ tsp.**	**2 mL**
Onion powder	**¼ tsp.**	**1 mL**
Salt	**½ tsp.**	**2 mL**
Pepper	**⅛ tsp.**	**0.5 mL**
Reserved chick pea liquid	**6 tbsp.**	**100 mL**

Parsley, for garnish
Crackers, bread cubes, raw vegetables or tortilla chips

Pour chick peas and lemon juice into blender. Process until smooth.

Add tahini, garlic powder, onion powder, salt and pepper. Process to mix. Add reserved liquid as needed to thin so it is like soft whipped cream. Can be served in bowl or on bed of lettuce.

Garnish with parsley. Serve with crackers, bread, raw vegetables or tortilla chips. Makes 2½ cups (625 mL).

TAHINI

This sesame spread works well on its own or in recipes such as Hummus, above.

Sesame seeds	**½ cup**	**125 mL**
Water	**¼ cup**	**60 mL**
Cooking oil	**2 tbsp.**	**30 mL**

Spread sesame seeds in ungreased jelly roll pan or larger pan. Toast in 350°F (175°C) oven for 5 to 10 minutes. Stir seeds every 2 minutes. The idea is to brown, not blacken, seeds. Place in blender.

Add water and cooking oil. Process about 3 minutes until smooth. Makes ½ cup (125 mL).

TIP

Make dip the day before serving to allow flavors to meld and texture to set. Keep chilled but serve dips at room temperature.

GARBANZO PÂTÉ

A soft pâté. Serve with crackers and ripe olives.

Cooking oil	2 tbsp.	30 mL
Chopped onion	1 cup	250 mL
Small green pepper, chopped	1	1
Chopped celery	1/3 cup	75 mL
Canned garbanzo beans (chick peas), drained	14 oz.	398 mL
Lemon juice, fresh or bottled	4 tsp.	20 mL
Whole oregano	1 tsp.	5 mL
Garlic powder	1/4 tsp.	1 mL
Salt	1/2 tsp.	2 mL
Pepper	1/8 tsp.	0.5 mL
Black olives, for garnish		

Heat cooking oil in frying pan. Add onion, green pepper and celery. Sauté 10 to 15 minutes until soft.

Combine next 6 ingredients in blender or food processor. Add onion mixture. Process until smooth. When serving, garnish with black olives. Makes 1 3/4 cups (425 mL).

Pictured below.

MEXICAN BEAN DIP

No need to travel to get a good dip. Guests will devour this in no time.

Cream cheese, softened	8 oz.	250 g
Sour cream	1 cup	250 mL
Refried beans	14 oz.	398 mL
Dry onion flakes	1 tbsp.	15 mL
Chives	1 tbsp.	15 mL
Parsley flakes	1 tbsp.	15 mL
Chili powder	2 tbsp.	30 mL
Grated medium or sharp Cheddar cheese	1½ cups	375 mL
Grated Monterey Jack cheese	1½ cups	375 mL
Chili powder, generous measure	2 tbsp.	30 mL

Green olives, for garnish

Mix first 7 ingredients in bowl. Spread in ungreased 3 quart
(3 L) casserole so it won't be too deep.

Sprinkle with Cheddar cheese then Monterey Jack cheese. Sprinkle
second amount of chili powder over top. May be chilled at this point
until needed. Bake, uncovered, in 350°F (175°C) oven for about
20 minutes until hot.

Garnish with green olives. Serve with assorted crackers.

Pictured on this page.

More people have discovered that vegetarian-style cooking makes a nice change to their usual daily fare. Here are some excellent suggestions for your next meal that feature all the nutritional benefits of a recipe containing meat, but without excess fat or cholesterol.

WHITE BEAN SAUSAGES

These fit right in to complete a meal. Excellent flavor.

Canned white kidney beans, drained	**19 oz.**	**540 mL**
Large egg	**1**	**1**
Ground sage	**½ tsp.**	**2 mL**
Salt	**½ tsp.**	**2 mL**
Pepper	**⅛ tsp.**	**0.5 mL**
Dry bread crumbs	**1 cup**	**250 mL**
Milk	**1 tbsp.**	**15 mL**
Cooking oil	**1 tbsp.**	**15 mL**

Mash beans on large plate with fork. Set aside.

Beat egg in bowl. Mix in sage, salt and pepper. Add bread crumbs. Stir. Add mashed beans. Mix well. Add a bit of milk if needed, just so mixture can be shaped. Shape into sausage rolls using about 2 tbsp. (30 mL) for each.

Heat cooking oil in frying pan. Brown sausages well on all sides. Add more cooking oil as needed. Makes 18.

TAMALE PIE

A bright yellow topping over a dark reddish filling.

Cooking oil	1 tbsp.	15 mL
Chopped onion	1 cup	250 mL
Chopped green pepper	½ cup	125 mL
Garlic clove, minced (or ¼ tsp., 1 mL, garlic powder)	1	1
Canned tomatoes, with juice, mashed	14 oz.	398 mL
Canned Romano beans, drained and mashed	19 oz.	540 mL
Bulgur	⅔ cup	150 mL
Ketchup	2 tbsp.	30 mL
Chili powder	1 tbsp.	15 mL
Salt	1 tsp.	5 mL
Pepper	¼ tsp.	1 mL
CRUST		
Yellow cornmeal	1 cup	250 mL
Baking powder	1 tsp.	5 mL
Salt	½ tsp.	2 mL
Large egg, fork-beaten	1	1
Milk	¾ cup	175 mL
Cooking oil	2 tbsp.	30 mL

Heat cooking oil in frying pan. Add onion, green pepper and garlic. Sauté until soft.

Add next 7 ingredients. Heat and stir until mixture boils. Cover and boil slowly for about 15 minutes. Stir often to keep from burning. It is quite thick. Turn into ungreased 8 x 8 inch (20 x 20 cm) pan. Set aside.

Crust: Stir cornmeal, baking powder and salt together in bowl. Add egg, milk and cooking oil. Stir. Pour over top. Bake, uncovered, in 350°F (175°C) oven for about 35 minutes until firm. Serves 6.

TIP

Simmer dried beans, rather than boiling. Stir gently to prevent skins from bursting.

VEGGIE STEW

A potful of beans and vegetables. Add spices to suit your taste.

Canned kidney beans, drained and liquid reserved	14 oz.	398 mL
Canned small white beans, drained and liquid reserved	19 oz.	540 mL
Canned chick peas (garbanzo beans), drained and liquid reserved	19 oz.	540 mL
Reserved liquids		
Water	1 cup	250 mL
Medium potatoes, cubed	2	2
Medium carrots, cubed	2	2
Cubed turnip	1 cup	250 mL
Chopped onion	2 cups	500 mL
Grated cabbage, packed	1 cup	250 mL
Thinly sliced celery	½ cup	125 mL
Soy sauce	2 tbsp.	30 mL
Bay leaves	2	2
Instant vegetable stock mix	2 tsp.	10 mL
Garlic powder	¼-1 tsp.	1-5 mL
Ground thyme	¼-1 tsp.	1-5 mL
Ground marjoram	¼-1 tsp.	1-5 mL
Ground cumin	⅛-¼ tsp.	0.5-1 mL
Salt	1 tsp.	5 mL
Pepper	¼ tsp.	1 mL
Canned stewed tomatoes, mashed	14 oz.	398 mL
Peas, fresh or frozen	1 cup	250 mL
Cornstarch	3 tbsp.	50 mL
Water	3 tbsp.	50 mL

(continued on next page)

PARÉ
pointer

Nobody shelves as

many ideas as a

librarian.

Combine beans in medium bowl. Set aside.

Combine next 17 ingredients in Dutch oven using least quantity of seasonings. Cover and simmer for 10 minutes. Add beans. Continue to simmer about 3 minutes more until vegetables are tender-crisp.

Add tomatoes and peas. Boil 3 to 4 minutes. Taste. Add more seasoning if desired.

Stir cornstarch into last amount of water in small cup. Stir into boiling stew until it returns to a boil and thickens slightly. Discard bay leaves. Makes 12 cups (3 L).

Pictured below.

Kidney beans and pasta go so well together. Use any pasta you have on hand and just substitute an equal measure into the recipe. Even spaghetti broken into little pieces works well. Leftovers keep for several days in the refrigerator, but avoid freezing once you have added your pasta because it will change in texture, becoming mushy and grainy.

PASTA WITH BEAN SAUCE

Serve with a salad and dinner roll and you've got a meal. Very good.

Elbow macaroni	2 cups	500 mL
Boiling water	2½ qts.	2.5 L
Cooking oil (optional)	1 tbsp.	15 mL
Salt	2 tsp.	10 mL
Chopped onion	1 cup	250 mL
Chopped green pepper	¼ cup	60 mL
Butter or hard margarine	2 tbsp.	30 mL
Canned kidney beans, drained	14 oz.	398 mL
Canned tomatoes, with juice, broken up	14 oz.	398 mL
Tomato sauce	7½ oz.	213 mL
Dried sweet basil	½ tsp.	2 mL
Ground marjoram	½ tsp.	2 mL
Ground oregano	½ tsp.	2 mL
Salt	½ tsp.	2 mL
Grated medium Cheddar cheese	1 cup	250 mL

Cook macaroni in boiling water, cooking oil and first amount of salt in uncovered large saucepan for 5 to 7 minutes until tender but firm. Drain. Return macaroni to saucepan.

While macaroni cooks, sauté onion and green pepper in butter in large saucepan until soft.

Add remaining ingredients. Heat, stirring often, until hot and cheese is melted. Stir into macaroni. Makes about 10 cups (2.5 L).

PARÉ
pointer

You will find that

when you use a

pogo stick it makes

you jumpy.

BEAN-SAUCED PASTA

A meal in one plateful.

TOMATO BEAN SAUCE

Cooking oil	1 tbsp.	15 mL
Chopped onion	1 cup	250 mL
Small green pepper, chopped	1	1
Garlic clove, minced (or ¼ tsp., 1 mL, garlic powder)	1	1
Canned stewed tomatoes, broken up	14 oz.	398 mL
Canned kidney beans, drained	14 oz.	398 mL
Apple juice	½ cup	125 mL
Salt	¼ tsp.	1 mL
Pepper	⅛ tsp.	0.5 mL
Liquid smoke	⅛-¼ tsp.	0.5-1 mL
PASTA		
Rigatoni or penne (tube pasta)	1 lb.	454 g
Boiling water	4 qts.	4 L
Cooking oil (optional)	1 tbsp.	15 mL
Salt	1 tbsp.	15 mL

Tomato Bean Sauce: Heat cooking oil in frying pan. Add onion, green pepper and garlic. Sauté until soft.

Add tomatoes, kidney beans, apple juice, salt and pepper. Stir. Add lesser amount of liquid smoke. Stir and taste. Add more if desired. Boil slowly for about 30 minutes until mixture gets slightly thicker.

Pasta: Cook rigatoni in boiling water, cooking oil and salt in large uncovered pot for 11 to 13 minutes until tender but firm. Drain. Divide among 4 warm plates. Divide sauce over top. Serves 4.

Pictured on this page.

CHILI BEAN PASTA

Protein galore! And so very good. Add more chili powder if you like.

Butter or hard margarine	2 tbsp.	30 mL
Chopped onion	1¼ cups	300 mL
Chopped green pepper	⅓ cup	75 mL
Canned tomatoes, with juice, mashed	14 oz.	398 mL
Canned kidney beans, drained	14 oz.	398 mL
Tomato sauce	7½ oz.	213 mL
Grated Cheddar cheese	2 cups	500 mL
Chili powder	2 tsp.	10 mL
Worcestershire sauce	1 tsp.	5 mL
Salt	½ tsp.	2 mL
Elbow macaroni	2 cups	500 mL
Boiling water	2½ qts.	2.5 L
Cooking oil (optional)	1 tbsp.	15 mL
Salt	2 tsp.	10 mL

Melt butter in large saucepan. Add onion and green pepper. Sauté until soft.

Add next 7 ingredients. Heat and stir until mixture simmers.

Cook macaroni in boiling water, cooking oil and second amount of salt in separate large uncovered saucepan for 5 to 7 minutes until tender but firm. Drain. Mix macaroni with sauce and serve. Makes about 10 cups (2.5 L).

Pictured on this page.

Add beans to a salad and you don't just have a side dish, you have a meal! Beans served in a salad can provide so much in terms of texture, color and nutrition, and these three delicious recipes help you do just that. Here's a suggestion—the next time you are serving a simple salad with dinner, try adding a can of kidney beans or chick peas for something a little different.

TACO SALAD

It's all here — protein, greens, crispness and good taste.

Lean ground raw chicken	1 lb.	454 g
Cooking oil	1 tbsp.	15 mL
Canned kidney beans, with liquid	14 oz.	398 mL
Envelope taco seasoning mix	1 × 1¼ oz.	1 × 35 g
Medium head of lettuce, cut up	1	1
Medium tomato, diced	1	1
Green onions, sliced	3	3
Peeled sliced cucumber	1 cup	250 mL
Ripe avocado, peeled, pitted and cut in cubes	1	1
Pimiento stuffed olives, halved	12	12
Grated medium Cheddar cheese	½ cup	125 mL
Bag of plain tortilla chips, crumbled	6 oz.	170 g
Thousand Island dressing	1 cup	250 mL

Scramble-fry chicken in cooking oil in frying pan until browned.

Stir in kidney beans and taco seasoning. Cool.

Toss next 7 ingredients together in large bowl.

Just before serving add chicken mixture and toss. Mix in tortilla chips and dressing. Toss lightly. Serves 10.

CORN CHIP SALAD

Crunchy with the taste of corn chips. Chili powder adds an extra touch along with the dressing.

Small head of lettuce, cut or torn	1	1
Grated medium or sharp Cheddar cheese	2 cups	500 mL
Medium tomatoes, diced and drained on paper towel	2	2
Green onions, sliced	3-4	3-4
Canned ranch-style beans (or kidney beans), drained and rinsed	½ × 14 oz.	½ × 398 mL
Chili powder	1 tsp.	5 mL
ISLAND DRESSING		
Cooking oil	1 tbsp.	15 mL
All-purpose flour	1 tbsp.	15 mL
Water	3 tbsp.	50 mL
White vinegar	2 tbsp.	30 mL
Granulated sugar	¼ cup	60 mL
Ketchup	2 tsp.	10 mL
Onion powder	⅛ tsp.	0.5 mL
Salt	⅛ tsp.	0.5 mL
Corn chips	3 cups	750 mL

Combine first 6 ingredients in large bowl. Toss.

Island Dressing: Stir cooking oil and flour together in small saucepan.

Stir in remaining ingredients. Heat and stir until mixture boils and thickens. Cool thoroughly before using. Makes ½ cup (125 mL). Add to salad. Toss well to coat. Chill for 30 minutes.

Add corn chips just before serving. Toss. Makes 10 cups (2.5 L).

Pictured on page 31.

PARÉ
pointer

The favorite dessert

of sculptors is

marble cake of

course.

OVERNIGHT BEAN SALAD

Crunchy, colorful, good flavor and a real lifesaver to have on hand.
Keeps for weeks in the refrigerator.

Canned yellow wax beans, drained	14 oz.	398 mL
Canned cut green beans, drained	14 oz.	398 mL
Canned kidney beans, drained	14 oz.	398 mL
Canned chick peas (garbanzo beans), drained	19 oz.	540 mL
Large onion, sliced	1	1
Red pepper, sliced in strips	1	1
DRESSING		
Granulated sugar	1 cup	250 mL
Red wine vinegar	¾ cup	175 mL
Cooking oil	2 tbsp.	30 mL
Salt	1 tsp.	5 mL
Pepper	½ tsp.	2 mL

Combine first 6 ingredients in bowl.

Dressing: Stir all 5 ingredients together well in separate bowl. Pour over bean mixture. Stir gently. Cover. Refrigerate overnight. Stir occasionally in evening and next morning. Makes 9 cups (2.2 L).

Pictured on front cover.

Corn Chip Salad, page 30

We know that traditional burgers and meat-filled sandwiches are high in fat, but we love them anyway. Perhaps that is why meatless burgers have become so popular. They allow us to indulge, guilt-free, in the great flavor of a burger without all the fat and cholesterol that traditionally comes with it. When you are preparing these recipes, consider using canned beans instead of cooked, dried beans as they are easier to form into patties.

CHICK PEA PATTIES

Lightly flavored with Parmesan cheese. More may be added if desired.

Bulgur	½ cup	125 mL
Boiling water	½ cup	125 mL
Large eggs	2	2
Canned chick peas (garbanzo beans), drained	19 oz.	540 mL
Dry bread crumbs	¼ cup	60 mL
Chopped fresh parsley (or 2 tsp., 10 mL, flakes)	3 tbsp.	50 mL
Grated Parmesan cheese	2 tbsp.	30 mL
Worcestershire sauce	1 tsp.	5 mL
Dry mustard powder	½ tsp.	2 mL
Salt	½ tsp.	2 mL
Whole oregano	¼ tsp.	1 mL
Dried sweet basil	¼ tsp.	1 mL
Garlic powder	¼ tsp.	1 mL
Pepper	⅛ tsp.	0.5 mL

Stir bulgur into boiling water in medium bowl. Cover. Let stand for 15 minutes.

Process eggs and chick peas in blender until smooth. Pour into bulgur. Stir.

Add remaining ingredients. Stir well. Shape into patties using ¼ cup (60 mL) for each. Fry in greased frying pan, browning both sides. Makes 10.

PARÉ *pointer*

When geese collide in mid-air, they get goose bumps.

BURRITOS

These are flavorful on their own but with salsa and sour cream they are extra good and spiced just right.

Cooking oil	2 tsp.	10 mL
Chopped onion	1¼ cups	300 mL
Garlic cloves, minced (or ½ tsp., 2 mL, garlic powder)	2	2
Medium potatoes, quartered	2	2
Boiling water, to cover		
Canned kidney beans (or pinto beans), drained	14 oz.	398 mL
Whole oregano	½ tsp.	2 mL
Ground cumin	½ tsp.	2 mL
Salt	½ tsp.	2 mL
Pepper	⅛ tsp.	0.5 mL
Flour tortillas, 8 inch (20 cm)	6	6
Salsa (mild, medium or hot)		
Sour cream		

Heat cooking oil in frying pan. Add onion and garlic. Sauté until soft and golden. Remove from heat.

Cook potatoes in boiling water until tender-crisp when pierced with tip of paring knife. Cool enough to handle. Cut into small dice. Add to onion.

Empty kidney beans into shallow pan or bowl. Add oregano, cumin, salt and pepper. Using bottom of water glass, mash well. Add to onion. Heat onion mixture, stirring often.

Wrap tortillas in foil. Heat in 350°F (175°C) oven for 8 to 10 minutes. Divide bean mixture down centers of tortillas. Fold 1 side over, then ends, then roll. Filling should be completely enclosed. If not serving immediately, wrap in foil and place in 200°F (95°C) oven.

Serve with salsa and sour cream. Makes 6 burritos.

Pictured on page 35.

PROTEIN BURGERS

Basil adds to the flavor of these. A slightly chewy texture.

Boiling water	¼ cup	60 mL
Bulgur	¼ cup	60 mL
Red lentils	3 tbsp.	50 mL
Boiling water, to cover		
Cooked dried navy beans (measure after cooking), see Note	1¾ cups	425 mL
Butter or hard margarine	1½ tbsp.	25 mL
Chopped onion	1¼ cups	300 mL
Dried sweet basil	1 tsp.	5 mL
Salt	¾ tsp.	4 mL
Pepper	⅛ tsp.	0.5 mL
Garlic powder	¼ tsp.	1 mL
Gravy browner	1 tsp.	5 mL
Hamburger buns, split and buttered	8	8

Pour first amount of boiling water over bulgur in small bowl. Cover. Let stand 15 minutes.

Cook lentils in second amount of boiling water until tender. Drain.

Add beans to lentils. Mash with bottom of drinking glass.

Heat butter in frying pan. Add onion. Sauté until soft. Turn into separate bowl.

Add remaining ingredients to onion. Mix. Add bulgur mixture and lentil mixture. Mix well. Shape into patties using about ¼ cup (60 mL) each. Brown both sides in greased frying pan.

Insert patties into buns. Serve as burgers with all the trimmings. Makes 8 burgers.

Note: Canned navy beans may be substituted if you don't have any cooked beans on hand. Use 14 oz. (398 mL).

Pictured on page 35.

PARÉ
pointer

To get the latest

headlines, sleep on a

corduroy pillow.

Clockwise from top left:
Protein Burgers, page 34; Burritos, page 33.

TOSTADOS

A toe-STAH-dah is a Mexican open-faced sandwich. Make tiny for hors d'œuvres and regular for first-course appetizers.

Flour tortillas (7 inch, 17.5 cm)	6	6
Cooking oil		
Canned refried beans	1 cup	250 mL
Salsa (mild, medium or hot)	6 tbsp.	100 mL
Grated Monterey Jack cheese	1 cup	250 mL
Shredded lettuce	2 cups	500 mL
Grated medium Cheddar cheese	½ cup	125 mL
Chopped green onion	2 tbsp.	30 mL

Fry tortillas in hot cooking oil in frying pan until crisp.

Divide remaining ingredients, in order given, among the 6 tortillas. Serves 6 as a sit-down appetizer or more if smaller tortillas are used.

TOSTADITOS: Use round tortilla chips. Make only ¼ or ½ recipe.

Pictured below.

PARÉ
pointer

Two fleas were
wondering if they
should walk home
or take the dog.

Like salads that include beans, a good bean soup is a delicious and hearty meal all by itself. Here are some great recipes that provide you with a variety of soups to choose from. If you want to make larger quantities and freeze your soup, undercook the vegetables so that they have a firmer texture when you thaw and reheat.

MINESTRONE

A full soup that becomes a full meal when served with crusty rolls.

Water	8 cups	2 L
Canned tomatoes, with juice, cut up	14 oz.	398 mL
Chopped onion	2¹/₂ cups	625 mL
Thinly sliced carrot	1 cup	250 mL
Thinly sliced celery	³/₄ cup	175 mL
Canned kidney beans, with liquid	14 oz.	398 mL
Cut green beans, fresh or frozen	2 cups	500 mL
Dry elbow macaroni	2 cups	500 mL
Instant vegetable stock mix	2 tbsp.	30 mL
Parsley flakes	2 tsp.	10 mL
Salt	1¹/₂ tsp.	7 mL
Pepper	¹/₄ tsp.	1 mL

Measure first 5 ingredients into Dutch oven. Heat, stirring often, until mixture comes to a boil. Cover. Simmer slowly for about 35 minutes until vegetables are cooked.

Add kidney beans and green beans. Return to a boil. Cook until green beans are tender.

Add macaroni, stock mix, parsley flakes, salt and pepper. Cover. Stir often as you return mixture to a boil. Cook for about 10 minutes until macaroni is tender but firm. Makes 13¹/₂ cups (3.37 L), enough for 12 servings.

BLACK BEAN SOUP

Soup at its darkest. Mild and tasty. Easy to double or triple recipe.

Water	1½ cups	375 mL
Canned black beans, with liquid	19 oz.	540 mL
Instant vegetable stock mix	4 tsp.	20 mL
Ground coriander	¼ tsp.	1 mL
Ground cumin	¼ tsp.	1 mL
Sweet pickle relish	1 tsp.	5 mL
Hot pepper sauce (add more if desired)	¼ tsp.	1 mL
Sour cream	2 tbsp.	30 mL
Grated Monterey Jack cheese	2 tsp.	10 mL

Run water and beans through blender. Pour into saucepan.

Add next 5 ingredients. Stir. Heat, stirring often, as mixture comes to a boil. Boil slowly, uncovered, for about 10 minutes to blend flavors.

Pour into 2 bowls. Top each with 1 tbsp. (15 mL) sour cream. Sprinkle each with 1 tsp. (5 mL) cheese. Makes 2 cups (500 mL).

Pictured on this page.

VEGETARIAN BEAN SOUP

Easy to make this thick soup. Good flavor. A real meal.

Dried white beans	2 cups	500 mL
Water	12 cups	3 L
Onion, chopped	1	1
Celery stalks, chopped	2	2
Carrot, finely diced	1	1
Canned tomatoes, with juice, broken up	14 oz.	398 mL
Medium potatoes, peeled and diced	2	2
Salt	2 tsp.	10 mL
Pepper	½ tsp.	2 mL
Parsley flakes	¼ tsp.	1 mL
Ground thyme	¼ tsp.	1 mL

(continued on next page)

Put beans and water in large pot. Bring to boil. Cover and simmer for 1½ to 2 hours until beans are tender.

Add remaining ingredients. Return to boil. Cover and simmer for about 15 minutes until vegetables are tender. Add more salt if needed. Serve hot. Makes about 10 cups (2.5 L).

Pictured on front cover.

PINTO TORTILLA SOUP

An excellent soup. Rich and hearty-looking. Mild salsa makes it spicy hot. A real winner.

Butter or hard margarine	1 tbsp.	15 mL
Chopped onion	½ cup	125 mL
Minced garlic	1 tsp.	5 mL
Water	3 cups	750 mL
Salsa, mild (or medium if you dare)	3 cups	750 mL
Canned pinto beans, with liquid	2 x 14 oz.	2 x 398 mL
Chopped red pepper	½ cup	125 mL
Bay leaf	1	1
Instant vegetable stock mix	2 tbsp.	30 mL
Pepper	¼ tsp.	1 mL
GARNISH		
Flour tortillas (any size), cut in 1½ x ¾ inch (4 x 2 cm) strips	2-3	2-3
Cooking oil, for deep-frying		
Grated medium Cheddar cheese or Monterey Jack cheese	½ cup	125 mL

Melt butter in saucepan. Add onion and garlic. Sauté until soft.

Add next 7 ingredients. Simmer, covered, for 1 hour. Discard bay leaf.

Garnish: Cook tortilla strips in hot 375°F (190°C) cooking oil until browned. Drain on paper towels.

Add some cheese and tortilla strips to each bowl of soup, if desired. Makes about 8½ cups (2.1 L), enough for 8 servings.

Pictured on this page.

GARBANZO SOUP

This has its own good flavor. Great choice.

Cooking oil	2 tbsp.	30 mL
Chopped onion	1½ cups	375 mL
Canned tomatoes, with juice, broken up	14 oz.	398 mL
Ketchup	2 tbsp.	30 mL
Instant vegetable stock mix	2 tbsp.	30 mL
Whole oregano	1 tsp.	5 mL
Garlic powder	¼ tsp.	1 mL
Salt	½ tsp.	2 mL
Pepper	⅛ tsp.	0.5 mL
Cayenne pepper	⅛ tsp.	0.5 mL
Water	3 cups	750 mL
Canned garbanzo beans (chick peas), with liquid, puréed in blender	19 oz.	540 mL
Plain yogurt or sour cream, per serving	1 tbsp.	15 mL

Heat cooking oil in large saucepan. Add onion. Sauté until soft.

Add next 9 ingredients. Heat, stirring often, until mixture comes to a boil. Boil gently for 15 minutes.

Add garbanzo purée. Stir. Return to a boil. Boil slowly for about 10 minutes to blend flavors well.

Add yogurt to center of each dish. Makes 6 cups (1.5 L).

PARÉ
pointer

A farmer minds his

peas. An actor

minds his cues.

It's always convenient to have a few recipes on hand that can be prepared at the last minute. Both these recipes cook quickly on the top of the stove and can be served with rice, potatoes or pasta.

HODGE PODGE

From the Maritimes and a garden filled with fresh vegetables. Amounts may vary according to vegetable preference and seasoning preference.

Medium potatoes, with peel, quartered	6	6
Sliced onion (optional)	1 cup	250 mL
Boiling water, to barely cover		
Salt		
Carrots, cut bite size	1 cup	250 mL
Fresh green string beans, cut up	1 cup	250 mL
Fresh yellow wax beans, cut up	1 cup	250 mL
Peas, fresh or frozen	1 cup	250 mL
Butter or hard margarine, softened	2-4 tbsp.	30-60 mL
Cream	1/4 cup	60 mL
Salt, sprinkle		
Pepper, sprinkle		

Cook potatoes and onion in boiling water and salt in large pot for about 10 minutes until half cooked.

Add remaining vegetables. Cook until tender. Drain.

Add butter, cream, salt and pepper. Toss to mix. Serves 6.

VEGETABLE STIR-FRY

String beans, mushrooms and green onions sautéed in a light sauce.
Tastes good.

Cut fresh green beans, parboiled 5 minutes	1 cup	250 mL
Sliced fresh mushrooms	1 cup	250 mL
Green onions, sliced	4	4
Cooking oil	1 tbsp.	15 mL
Soy sauce	1 tbsp.	15 mL
Salt	¼ tsp.	1 mL
Garlic powder	¼ tsp.	1 mL
Ground ginger	⅛ tsp.	0.5 mL
Slivered almonds, toasted in 350°F (175°C) oven for 5 to 10 minutes until lightly browned	¼ cup	60 mL

Stir-fry beans, mushrooms and onion in cooking oil in wok or frying pan for 4 to 5 minutes.

Stir in remaining ingredients. Serves 2.

Pictured below.

Glossary of Rice

TYPE OF RICE	SIZE	FLAVOR	COOKED TEXTURE
Arborio	Short grain	Mild	Soft with creamy sauce
Basmati	Long slender grain	Very fragrant	Stays separated
Brown	Medium-long grain	Earthy, nutty	Chewy
Jasmine	Long grain	Aromatic, nutty	Soft
Parboiled (converted)	Long grain	Mild	Firm, stays separated
Pearl	Short grain	Mild	Soft & sticky
Regular	Long grain	Mild	Soft
Wild	Very long slender grain	Nutty	Chewy

Rice has always been an excellent ingredient for stuffings and fillings, whether in a roast chicken or cherry tomato appetizer! To save time, make your rice the day before and chill, then use as directed in the recipe. Rice can also be made well in advance and frozen. Thaw and reheat slowly, covered, to bring back the smooth texture.

RICE-STUFFED TOMATOES

Looks good and tastes good. Cheese adds much to the flavor. Makes good finger food if using cherry tomatoes.

Firm ripe tomatoes	6	6
Reserved tomato pulp		
Cooked white rice	2 cups	500 mL
Granulated sugar	1/2 tsp.	2 mL
Salt	3/4 tsp.	4 mL
Pepper	1/4 tsp.	1 mL
Dried sweet basil	1/4 tsp.	1 mL
Ground oregano	1/8 tsp.	0.5 mL
Garlic powder	1/8 tsp.	0.5 mL
Parsley flakes	1/2 tsp.	2 mL
Grated medium Cheddar cheese	1/2 cup	125 mL

Cut off tops from tomatoes. Scoop out pulp and reserve.

Mash reserved tomato pulp. Add remaining ingredients. Mix together. Stuff tomatoes. Arrange in greased baking pan. Bake, uncovered, in 350°F (175°C) oven for 20 to 25 minutes. Serves 6.

STUFFED CHERRY TOMATOES

Elegant showpieces on an appetizer tray.

Cherry tomatoes	**2 cups**	**500 mL**
Salt, sprinkle		
RICE FILLING		
Cooked white rice	**1 cup**	**250 mL**
Green onions, finely chopped	**1-2**	**1-2**
Chopped nuts (optional)	**1 tbsp.**	**15 mL**
Worcestershire sauce	**¹⁄₈ tsp.**	**0.5 mL**
Salad dressing (or mayonnaise)	**1 tbsp.**	**15 mL**

Cut tops from tomatoes. Scoop out some of the pulp. Sprinkle inside with salt. Place tomatoes upside down on paper towel to drain for ¹⁄₂ hour. Top may be used as a lid after stuffing tomato. Or tomato may be cut almost to the bottom to make 4 or 6 petals.

Rice Filling: Combine all 5 ingredients. Add more salad dressing if needed. Overstuff tomatoes. Replace tops, if using. Makes about 12.

RICE STUFFING

Easy, moist and delicious. Will stuff 4 to 5 Cornish hens or 1 chicken.

Long grain white rice, uncooked	**1¹⁄₂ cups**	**375 mL**
Chopped onion	**³⁄₄ cup**	**175 mL**
Chopped celery	**¹⁄₂ cup**	**125 mL**
Sliced fresh mushrooms	**¹⁄₂ cup**	**125 mL**
Salt	**1 tsp.**	**5 mL**
Ground thyme	**¹⁄₄ tsp.**	**1 mL**
Ground sage	**¹⁄₈ tsp.**	**0.5 mL**
Boiling water	**3 cups**	**750 mL**
Butter or hard margarine	**4 tbsp.**	**60 mL**

Measure first 8 ingredients into medium saucepan. Stir. Bring to a boil. Simmer, covered, for about 15 minutes until rice is tender and water is absorbed.

Stir in butter until it melts. Cool for several minutes. Makes about 5 cups (1.2 L).

Here is where the versatility of rice really shows! As a main course, rice can be served in a casserole, rolled in cabbage, or even shaped into a pizza crust. These recipes can be frozen ahead of time for convenience—simply reheat, covered, to "steam" or plump up the rice.

SAUSAGE RICE CASSEROLE

Have this ready to serve when the gang gets back from skiing, skating or tobogganing.

Long grain white rice	1 cup	250 mL
Chopped onion	1 cup	250 mL
Salt	½ tsp.	2 mL
Boiling water	2 cups	500 mL
Sausage meat	1 lb.	454 g
Condensed cream of tomato soup	10 oz.	284 mL
Milk or water (use can to measure)	10 oz.	284 mL
Grated medium or sharp Cheddar cheese	1 cup	250 mL

Cook rice and onion in salt and boiling water for about 20 minutes until tender and water is absorbed.

Shape sausage meat into 1 inch (2.5 cm) balls. Flatten each ball into a tiny patty. Fry, browning both sides, until no pink remains in meat.

Whisk soup and milk together in bowl until smooth. Layer ½ the rice in bottom of ungreased 2 quart (2 L) casserole. Pour ½ soup mixture over rice. Add second ½ rice. Cover in single layer, with sausage patties. Pour remaining ½ soup mixture over patties.

Sprinkle with cheese. Bake in 350°F (175°C) oven for 35 to 45 minutes until bubbly hot. Serves 4 to 6.

LAZY CABBAGE ROLLS

No trick at all to these. Easy to make. Use canned sauerkraut or your own.

Long grain white rice	**1½ cups**	**375 mL**
Water	**1½ cups**	**375 mL**
Salt	**1 tsp.**	**5 mL**
Bacon slices, chopped	**4**	**4**
Chopped onion	**½ cup**	**125 mL**
Canned sauerkraut, drained	**19 oz.**	**540 mL**

Put rice, water and salt into saucepan. Cover. Bring to a boil. Simmer for about 15 minutes until rice is tender and water is absorbed.

Sauté bacon and onion together in frying pan until onion is soft and clear.

Add sauerkraut. Stir. Add rice. Mix together. Turn into greased 2 quart (2 L) casserole. Cover. Bake in 350°F (175°C) oven for about 45 minutes.

Pictured below.

CURRIED HAM ROLLS

Nice for a lighter meal or for a second meat.

CURRY SAUCE

Butter or hard margarine	¼ cup	60 mL
All-purpose flour	¼ cup	60 mL
Curry powder	2 tsp.	10 mL
Salt	1 tsp.	5 mL
Milk	2 cups	500 mL
Raisins	1 cup	250 mL

ROLLS

Cooked white rice	2 cups	500 mL
Curry Sauce (above)	½ cup	125 mL
Finely chopped onion	2 tbsp.	30 mL
Parsley flakes	1 tsp.	5 mL
Ham slices, ⅛ inch (0.5 cm) thick	12	12

Curry Sauce: Melt butter in saucepan. Mix in flour, curry powder, and salt. Stir in milk and raisins until sauce boils and thickens.

Rolls: Mix rice, Curry Sauce, onion and parsley together.

Divide rice mixture and spread on ham slices. If using very thin sandwich-type ham, use 2 to 3 to obtain desired thickness. Roll up and place in shallow greased baking dish, seam side down. Spoon remaining Curry Sauce over top adding a bit more milk if desired. Bake, uncovered, in 325°F (160°C) oven for 25 to 30 minutes until heated through. Makes 12 rolls.

Pictured on page 49.

PARÉ
pointer

A tailor's son is a

son of a sew and

sew.

Top: Chicken Rice Bake, page 51
Bottom: Curried Ham Rolls, page 48

PINEAPPLE HAM PIZZA

This has a rice crust covered with cheese, ham and pineapple, and uses low-fat ingredients.

RICE CRUST

Long grain white rice	½ cup	125 mL
Boiling water	1 cup	250 mL
All-purpose flour	1½ cups	375 mL
Fast rising instant yeast	1½ tsp.	7 mL
Warm water	½ cup	125 mL

TOPPING

Tomato paste	½ × 5½ oz.	½ × 156 mL
Water	⅓ cup	75 mL
Onion powder	¼ tsp.	1 mL
Ground oregano	¼ tsp.	1 mL
Liquid sweetener	¼ tsp.	1 mL
Dried sweet basil	¼ tsp.	1 mL
Garlic salt	½ tsp.	2 mL
Grated part-skim mozzarella cheese (35% less fat)	¾ cup	175 mL
Unsweetened pineapple tidbits, drained	14 oz.	398 mL
Ham cubes	⅔ cup	150 mL
Green pepper, cut in slivers	½	½
Grated part-skim mozzarella cheese (35% less fat)	¾ cup	175 mL
Grated low-fat medium or sharp Cheddar cheese (less than 21% MF)	½ cup	125 mL

PARÉ
pointer

A boy who takes a bath without being told is probably giving the dog one.

Rice Crust: Cook rice in boiling water until tender and water is absorbed. Measure 1¼ cups (300 mL) into bowl. Cool a little.

Add flour and yeast. Stir well. Add water. Mix. Knead 25 times on lightly floured surface mixing in a bit more flour if sticky. Roll and stretch to fit 12 inch (30 cm) pizza pan that has been sprayed with no-stick cooking spray.

(continued on next page)

Topping: Stir first 7 ingredients together. Spread over crust.

Sprinkle with first amount of mozzarella cheese, pineapple, ham and green pepper. Bake on bottom shelf of 450°F (230°C) oven for 20 minutes.

Sprinkle with second amount of mozzarella cheese. Add Cheddar cheese. Continue to bake for 5 to 10 minutes more until cheese is melted and crust is browned. Cut into 8 wedges.

CHICKEN RICE BAKE

Colorful with bits of pimiento and parsley showing.

Boneless chicken breasts, skin and fat removed	2 lbs.	900 g
Paprika	½ tsp.	2 mL
Celery salt	½ tsp.	2 mL
Garlic powder	½ tsp.	2 mL
Boiling water	2 cups	500 mL
Chicken bouillon powder (35% less salt)	1 tbsp.	15 mL
Long grain white rice, uncooked	1 cup	250 mL
Chopped pimiento	2 tbsp.	30 mL
Parsley flakes	½ tsp.	2 mL

Spray frying pan with no-stick cooking spray. Brown chicken on each side, sprinkling with ½ mixture of paprika, celery salt and garlic powder. Turn and sprinkle with second ½ of mixture.

Pour water into 3 quart (3 L) casserole. Stir in bouillon powder. Add rice, pimiento and parsley. Stir. Lay chicken on top. Cover. Bake in 350°F (175°C) oven for about 1 hour until rice is tender, water is absorbed and chicken is cooked. Makes 8 servings.

Pictured on page 49.

TIP
Rice is one of the few cooked foods that can be refrigerated, covered, safely for up to 1 week.

BROCCOLI RICE BAKE

Both convenient and simple to make.

Butter or hard margarine	1 tbsp.	15 mL
Chopped onion	½ cup	125 mL
Chopped celery	¼ cup	60 mL
Broccoli, coarsely chopped	1 lb.	454 g
Boiling water		
Condensed cream of mushroom soup	10 oz.	284 mL
Soup can of water	10 oz.	284 mL
Soup can of instant rice	10 oz.	284 mL
Grated medium or sharp Cheddar cheese	½ cup	125 mL
Worcestershire sauce	1 tsp.	5 mL
Ground thyme	⅛ tsp.	0.5 mL
Cayenne pepper	⅛ tsp.	0.5 mL
Grated medium or sharp Cheddar cheese	¼ cup	60 mL

Melt butter in frying pan. Add onion and celery. Sauté until soft.

Cook broccoli in boiling water until tender-crisp. Drain.

Mix next 7 ingredients in a large bowl. Add vegetables. Stir. Turn into ungreased 2 quart (2 L) casserole.

Sprinkle with second amount of cheese. Cover. Bake in 350°F (175°C) oven for 30 to 35 minutes. Serves 6.

PARÉ
pointer

Liquid assets to a

teenager is a

refrigerator full of

soft drinks.

RICE VEGGIE CASSEROLE

One of the most colorful dishes you can make.

Medium onion, chopped	1	1
Sliced celery	1 cup	250 mL
Canned tomatoes, drained, chopped, drained again	19 oz.	540 mL
Chili powder	2 tsp.	10 mL
Green pepper, chopped	1	1
Canned kidney beans, drained	14 oz.	398 mL
Cooked brown rice (about ¼ cup, 60 mL, uncooked)	1 cup	250 mL
Canned kernel corn, drained	12 oz.	341 mL
Salt	¼ tsp.	1 mL
Pepper	⅛ tsp.	0.5 mL
Crumbled whole wheat crackers (or unsalted corn chips)	½ cup	125 mL
Grated Edam cheese	½ cup	125 mL

Combine first 4 ingredients in saucepan. Heat to a simmer. Cover and simmer for 5 minutes. Stir once or twice during cooking. Remove from heat.

Add next 6 ingredients. Stir. Pour into ungreased 2 quart (2 L) casserole. Cover. Bake in 350°F (175°C) oven for 15 minutes.

Sprinkle with crackers and cheese. Bake, uncovered, for another 15 minutes. Serves 6 people, 1 cup (250 mL) each.

Pictured on this page.

CHEESY RICE

Makes a large layered casserole. Great flavor.

Brown rice	2 cups	500 mL
Boiling water	4 cups	1 L
Salt	1 tsp.	5 mL
Butter or hard margarine	1½ tbsp.	25 mL
Chopped onion	1½ cups	375 mL
Canned black-eyed peas, drained	14 oz.	398 mL
Canned diced green chilies, drained	4 oz.	114 mL
Garlic powder	½ tsp.	2 mL
Parsley flakes	1 tsp.	5 mL
Pepper	¼ tsp.	1 mL
Grated Monterey Jack cheese	2 cups	500 mL
Creamed cottage cheese	2 cups	500 mL
Grated medium or sharp Cheddar cheese	¾ cup	175 mL

Cook rice in boiling water and salt for about 45 minutes until tender and water is absorbed.

Melt butter in frying pan. Add onion. Sauté until soft. Add to rice.

Add peas, green chilies, garlic powder, parsley and pepper. Stir.

Assemble in layers in ungreased 3 quart (3 L) casserole as follows:

1. ⅓ rice mixture
2. ½ Monterey Jack cheese
3. ½ cottage cheese
4. ⅓ rice mixture
5. ½ Monterey Jack cheese
6. ½ cottage cheese
7. ⅓ rice mixture
8. Cheddar cheese

Bake, covered, in 350°F (175°C) oven for about 1 hour until heated through and cheese is melted. If you would like to brown cheese a little, remove cover and bake 10 minutes more. Serves 8.

PARÉ
pointer

The harried parents

of quadruplets

exclaimed "Four

crying out loud!"

There are many varieties of traditional rice pudding that can be made, and here are a few recipes to demonstrate! When baked, rice pudding has a custard-like consistency, while cooking on stove-top results in a more pudding-like texture. It's best to serve rice pudding while still warm, so check each recipe carefully to determine your time frame for preparation. Enjoy these recipes as they are or serve with a little extra milk or cream.

RICE MERINGUE PUDDING

A top-of-the-stove dessert, finished in the oven with a golden crown.
Fast and easy.

Short grain white rice, uncooked	½ cup	125 mL
Milk	4 cups	1 L
Granulated sugar	½ cup	125 mL
Lemon juice, fresh or bottled	2 tsp.	10 mL
Salt	½ tsp.	2 mL
Egg yolks (large), fork-beaten	3	3
Vanilla	1 tsp.	5 mL
Egg whites (large), room temperature	3	3
Cream of tartar	¼ tsp.	1 mL
Granulated sugar	3 tbsp.	50 mL

Measure first 5 ingredients into large saucepan. Bring to a boil. Cover. Simmer slowly for about 15 minutes until rice is tender, stirring occasionally. Remove from heat.

Stir a bit of hot rice into egg yolks, then stir yolk mixture back into rice. Cook to thicken. Add vanilla. Spoon into ungreased 8 inch (20 cm) casserole. Smooth top.

Beat egg whites and cream of tartar until soft peaks form. Add sugar gradually, beating until stiff. Spread over top of hot rice mixture. Bake, uncovered, in 400°F (205°C) oven for 5 minutes or until lightly browned.

OVEN RICE PUDDING

A creamy pudding that needs very little watching. A real comfort food.

Milk	4 cups	1 L
Short grain white rice, uncooked	1/2 cup	125 mL
Granulated sugar	3 tbsp.	50 mL
Raisins	1/3 cup	75 mL
Vanilla	1 tsp.	5 mL
Salt	1/2 tsp.	2 mL
Cinnamon (optional but good)	1/4 tsp.	1 mL

Combine all ingredients in ungreased 8 inch (20 cm) casserole. The addition of cinnamon is delicious although the pudding will not be as white as it would be without it. Bake in 350°F (175°C) oven for about 1½ hours until rice is tender and pudding is creamy. Stir in the skin formation at least twice during baking time. Allow skin to remain for last part of cooking. Serve warm with or without table cream. Leftovers can be eaten cold. Serves 6 to 8.

Chocolate Rice Pudding, page 56

CREAMY RICE PUDDING

Makes a nice creamy dessert using leftover or freshly cooked rice.

Cooked white rice	1½ cups	375 mL
Milk	1½ cups	375 mL
Granulated sugar	1/4 cup	60 mL
Vanilla	1 tsp.	5 mL
Raisins	1/3 cup	75 mL
Butter or hard margarine	1 tbsp.	15 mL

Combine all 6 ingredients in top of double boiler. Cook over simmering water, stirring occasionally. When thickened, pour into serving bowl. Serve hot today and leftovers cold tomorrow. Serves 6.

CREAMY RICE CUSTARD: Add 2 slightly beaten large eggs at the last. Stir continuously as it cooks until mixture coats a metal spoon. Serves 6.

CHOCOLATE RICE PUDDING: Add 2 tbsp. (30 mL) cocoa.

Pictured on this page.

If you have never prepared a rice salad, this is the perfect time to start! Always popular and ready for any buffet, rice salads can offer a different flavor than traditional lettuce salads, from spicy oriental to summer sweet. Save some time by making your rice in advance and freezing, then reheat and use in any one of these quick and easy recipes.

BEST RICE SALAD

Do try this recipe. It is widely acclaimed.

Hot cooked white rice	2 cups	500 mL
Chopped celery	1½ cups	375 mL
Peas, fresh or frozen	1 cup	250 mL
Finely chopped green onion	¼ cup	60 mL
Canned small shrimp, rinsed and drained	4 oz.	113 g
Cooking oil	½ cup	125 mL
White vinegar	3 tbsp.	50 mL
Soy sauce	2 tbsp.	30 mL
Curry powder	1½-2 tsp.	7-10 mL
Salt	1 tsp.	5 mL
Granulated sugar	½ tsp.	2 mL
Celery salt	½ tsp.	2 mL

Put hot rice in bowl. Add celery, peas, onion and shrimp.

Mix next 7 ingredients in small bowl. Stir and pour over rice mixture. Stir lightly to coat. Serves 4 to 6.

TIP

White rice (short or long grain) can be stored in an airtight container indefinitely, while brown rice has a limited shelf life of a maximum of 3 months.

WILD RICE AND SEAFOOD SALAD

Shrimp and crab combined with rice, tossed with a different dressing. Zesty and tasty.

Box of long grain and wild rice mix	1 × 6¹/₂ oz.	1 × 170 g
Canned crabmeat, drained, membrane removed	4.2 oz.	120 g
Canned small shrimp, rinsed and drained	4 oz.	113 g
Chopped green onion	2 tbsp.	30 mL
DRESSING		
Salad dressing (or mayonnaise)	1 cup	250 mL
Red wine vinegar	2 tbsp.	30 mL
Prepared mustard	1 tsp.	5 mL
Prepared horseradish	1 tsp.	5 mL
Frilly lettuce leaves	6-12	6-12
Hard-boiled eggs, quartered lengthwise	3	3
Cherry tomatoes, quartered lengthwise	6	6

Cook rice mix according to package directions.

Combine crabmeat and shrimp in bowl. Add prepared rice and onion.

Dressing: Stir all 4 ingredients together in small bowl. Pour over rice mixture. Toss. Chill until ready to serve.

Cover 6 salad plates with lettuce. Divide seafood mixture over lettuce.

Arrange egg and tomato wedges around salad on each plate. Serves 6.

Pictured on this page.

TOMATO RICE SALAD

Good and colorful.

Long grain white rice	1 cup	250 mL
Boiling water	2 cups	500 mL
Salt	1 tsp.	5 mL
Tomatoes, peeled and chopped (see Note)	6	6
Sliced fresh mushrooms	1 cup	250 mL
Green onions, sliced	4	4
Chopped fresh parsley (or 1 tsp., 5 mL flakes)	2 tbsp.	30 mL
DRESSING		
Cooking oil	¼ cup	60 mL
Lemon juice, fresh or bottled	¼ cup	60 mL
Garlic salt	¼ tsp.	1 mL
Prepared mustard	1 tsp.	5 mL
Dried sweet basil	½ tsp.	2 mL
Granulated sugar	2 tsp.	10 mL
Salt	1 tsp.	5 mL
Pepper	¼ tsp.	1 mL

Cook rice in boiling water and salt until tender and water is absorbed. Rinse with cold water. Drain well.

Combine tomatoes, mushrooms, onion and parsley in large bowl. Add rice. Mix.

Dressing: Mix all 8 ingredients together in small bowl. Pour about ⅔ dressing over salad ingredients. Toss. Add more dressing as needed. Serves 8.

Note: To peel tomatoes, dip in boiling water for about 1 minute.

PARÉ
pointer

When grapes worry,

they wrinkle and

turn into raisins.

GLORIFIED RICE

Dress up leftover rice with colored marshmallows, pineapple and whipped cream.

Cooked white rice	**1½ cups**	**375 mL**
Crushed pineapple, drained	**14 oz.**	**398 mL**
Miniature marshmallows	**1 cup**	**250 mL**
Whipping cream (or 1 env. topping)	**1 cup**	**250 mL**
Granulated sugar	**3 tbsp.**	**50 mL**
Vanilla	**1 tsp.**	**5 mL**

Maraschino cherries or slivered toasted almonds

Combine rice, pineapple and marshmallows in bowl.

Beat cream, sugar and vanilla until stiff. Fold into rice mixture.

Garnish with cherries or nuts. Chill at least 2 hours. Serves 6.

Pictured above.

Variation: Add ¼ cup (60 mL) each of chopped maraschino cherries and chopped nuts.

Variation: Omit pineapple. Add 14 oz. (398 mL) can of fruit cocktail, drained.

Many well-known seafood dishes include rice as an ingredient—here are some perfect examples for you to choose from. These casserole-style recipes are great for serving to dinner guests and are certain to please everyone with their subtle and satisfying flavor.

SALMON RICE BAKE

Contains carrot, onion, broccoli and rice to make a full meal-type casserole.

Water	3 cups	750 mL
Grated carrot, packed	1½ cups	375 mL
Finely chopped onion	1 cup	250 mL
Chicken bouillon powder (35% less salt)	2 tsp.	10 mL
Small broccoli florets	1 cup	250 mL
Instant rice, uncooked	2¼ cups	560 mL
Condensed cream of mushroom soup	10 oz.	284 mL
Canned pink salmon (no added salt), drained, skin and round bones removed	7½ oz.	213 g
Paprika, sprinkle		

Combine water, carrot, onion and bouillon powder in saucepan. Cover and cook until onion is almost tender.

Add broccoli. Cook for 4 minutes. Do not drain.

Stir in rice. Cover. Let stand 5 minutes.

Add soup. Stir to mix. Break up salmon. Stir in. Turn into greased 2 quart (2 L) casserole.

Sprinkle with paprika. Cover. Bake in 350°F (175°C) oven for 30 minutes. Makes 6⅓ cups (1.6 L).

PARÉ
pointer

Why is it children slam the doors in summer that they left open all winter?

PAELLA

Spanish in origin, pie-AY-yuh is a terrific company casserole. Serve with green peas for color contrast.

Cooking oil	2 tbsp.	30 mL
Boneless chicken breast halves	8	8
Chopped onion	1½ cups	375 mL
Garlic cloves, minced (or ½ tsp., 2 mL garlic powder)	2	2
Chorizo or other hot sausage, sliced ½ inch (12 mm) thick	¾ lb.	340 g
Water	4 cups	1 L
Canned stewed tomatoes	14 oz.	398 mL
Long grain white rice, uncooked	2 cups	500 mL
Chicken bouillon powder	4 tsp.	20 mL
Saffron (or turmeric)	¼ tsp.	1 mL
Salt	2 tsp.	10 mL
Pepper	½ tsp.	2 mL
Scallops (halve large ones)	1 lb.	454 g
Boiling water, to cover		
Medium uncooked shrimp, peeled and deveined	1 lb.	454 g
Boiling water, to cover		
Pimiento strips, for garnish		
Black olives, for garnish		

Heat cooking oil in Dutch oven. Add chicken in 1 or 2 batches. Brown both sides quickly. It is not necessary to cook it through at this stage. Remove chicken to plate. Cut into bite size pieces.

Add onion, garlic and sausage to Dutch oven, adding more cooking oil if needed. Sauté until onion is soft.

Add water, tomatoes, rice, bouillon powder, saffron, salt and pepper. Add chicken. Bring to a boil. Cover. Cook over medium heat for 15 to 20 minutes until rice is tender.

(continued on next page)

Cook scallops in first amount of boiling water for 3 to 5 minutes until white and opaque. Drain. Add to mixture in Dutch oven.

Cook shrimp in second amount of boiling water for about 1 minute until pinkish and curled. Drain. Add to mixture in Dutch oven.

Garnish with pimiento strips and olives. Serves 8.

Pictured below.

KINGFISH CASSEROLE

Very colorful with a cheese and paprika topping. An excellent meal to make in the microwave.

Instant rice	1½ cups	375 mL
Hot water	1½ cups	375 mL
Canned mushroom pieces, drained	10 oz.	284 mL
Dry onion flakes	1 tbsp.	15 mL
Chicken bouillon powder	2 tsp.	10 mL
Salt	½ tsp.	2 mL
Fish fillets	4	4
APPLE CREAM SAUCE		
Butter or hard margarine	2 tbsp.	30 mL
All-purpose flour	2 tbsp.	30 mL
Milk	1 cup	250 mL
Apple juice	⅓ cup	75 mL
Salt	¼ tsp.	1 mL
Paprika, sprinkle		
Grated medium Cheddar cheese	1 cup	250 mL

Measure first 6 ingredients into ungreased 2 quart (2 L) casserole. Stir. Cover. Microwave on high (100%) for about 5 minutes until mixture starts to boil and absorbs the liquid. Stir.

Lay fish fillets over top in single layer.

Apple Cream Sauce: Place butter in 2 cup (500 mL) measuring cup. Microwave, uncovered, on high (100%) about 40 seconds to melt.

Mix in flour. Add milk, apple juice and salt. Stir. Microwave, uncovered, on high (100%) for about 3 minutes, until sauce boils and thickens a little, stirring twice. Pour over fish. Cover with waxed paper. Microwave on high (100%) for about 7 minutes until fish flakes when tested with fork, rotating dish ½ turn at half time if you don't have a turntable.

Sprinkle with paprika and cheese. Microwave, uncovered, on high (100%) for about 2 minutes to melt cheese. Serves 4.

PARÉ
pointer

Bells are so easy to

manage. They

always sound off

when tolled.

SHRIMP AND RICE CREOLE

Good tomato flavor with lots of shrimp.

Long grain white rice	⅔ cup	150 mL
Boiling water	1⅓ cups	325 mL
Medium shrimp, shelled and deveined	1 lb.	454 g
Boiling water	1½ cups	375 mL
Chopped onion	½ cup	125 mL
Chopped green pepper	¼ cup	60 mL
Sliced fresh mushrooms	1 cup	250 mL
Tomato paste	5½ oz.	156 mL
Water	¾ cup	175 mL
Granulated sugar	1 tsp.	5 mL
Salt	½ tsp.	2 mL
Pepper	¼ tsp.	1 mL
TOPPING		
Hard margarine	1 tbsp.	15 mL
Dry bread crumbs	⅓ cup	75 mL

Cook rice in first amount of boiling water for about 15 minutes until tender and water is absorbed. Set aside.

Cook shrimp in second amount of boiling water for about 5 minutes until pinkish and curled a bit. Drain. Cut up into bite size pieces. Set aside.

Spray frying pan with no-stick cooking spray. Add onion, green pepper and mushrooms. Sauté until soft.

Mix tomato paste, third amount of water, sugar, salt and pepper in medium size bowl. Add prepared rice, shrimp and onion mixture. Stir. Turn into greased 1½ quart (1.5 L) casserole.

Topping: Melt margarine in small saucepan. Stir in bread crumbs. Spread over casserole. Bake, uncovered, in 350°F (175°C) oven for 30 minutes. Makes 5 cups (1.2 L).

Pictured on this page.

Soup is always a popular meal for any time of day. When you include rice in soup, the result is an economical and satisfying dish higher in carbohydrates and lower in fat. Make your selection from this delicious assortment of recipes and discover some great soups you will want to try again and again.

SEAFOOD GUMBO

A superb creation from southern Louisiana. It can contain leftovers of ham, turkey or chicken along with seafood. It is served over a mound of rice in a shallow bowl. Don't be intimidated by the length of the recipe. If time runs out, continue later. Gumbo is better the second day anyway.

Butter or hard margarine, melted	¼ cup	60 mL
All-purpose flour	2 tbsp.	30 mL
Large onion, chopped	1	1
Hot water	2 cups	500 mL
Chopped celery	¼ cup	60 mL
Chopped green pepper	¼ cup	60 mL
Canned tomatoes, with juice, mashed	14 oz.	398 mL
Canned okra, with liquid, sliced	14 oz.	398 mL
Granulated sugar	1 tsp.	5 mL
Salt	1 tsp.	5 mL
Pepper	¼ tsp.	1 mL
Garlic powder (or 1 clove, minced)	¼ tsp.	1 mL
Ground thyme	⅛ tsp.	0.5 mL
Cayenne pepper, sprinkle (optional)		
Shrimp, or crabmeat, or some of both (see Note)	4-6 cups	1-1.5 L
Hot cooked white rice	2 cups	500 mL
Green onions, sliced (optional)	2	2

First make a brown roux (roo) by stirring margarine and flour together in heavy large saucepan over medium heat until dark brown, the color of chocolate. This will take quite a few minutes. Do not scorch.

(continued on next page)

· P A R É
pointer

A bird that sits all the time is better known as a stool pigeon.

As soon as desired color is reached, stir in onion to reduce temperature and stop the browning. Add water, celery, green pepper, tomatoes, okra, sugar, salt, pepper, garlic powder and thyme. Sprinkle with cayenne pepper. The amount depends on how hot you want it. Bring to a boil. Cover and simmer for 30 to 45 minutes or longer, stirring occasionally.

Add shrimp and crabmeat. Add enough to make it thick.

Place mound of rice in each bowl. Sprinkle with green onion. Ladle soup into bowls. Serve with thick slices of garlic bread or crusty rolls. Makes about 6 cups (1.5 L).

Note: Tuna may be added in place of shrimp and crabmeat for bulk and economy.

GREEK LEMON SOUP

Avgolemono (AV-guh-LEM-on-oh) consists chiefly of rice cooked in broth with a slight lemon flavor. Popular in Greece. Do not freeze.

Chicken broth	6 cups	1.5 L
Long grain white rice	½ cup	125 mL
Large eggs	4	4
Lemon juice, fresh or bottled	4 tsp.	20 mL
Pepper, sprinkle (white is best)		
Chives or parsley, for garnish		

Put chicken stock and rice into large saucepan. Bring to a boil. Cover and simmer for about 15 minutes until rice is tender.

Beat eggs in medium bowl until frothy. Add lemon juice. Gradually stir in about ⅓ chicken-rice mixture. Add back to saucepan, stirring. Do not allow to return to simmer or it will curdle. Add a light sprinkle of pepper. Stir and taste before adding more. Garnish with chopped chives or chopped parsley. Makes about 6 cups (1.5 L).

Pictured on this page.

COCK-A-LEEKIE SOUP

Sure to bring out the Scotch in anyone. A full-bodied soup.

Chicken stock (see Note)	**10 cups**	**2.5 L**
Leeks, white part only, chopped	**8**	**8**
Long grain white rice, uncooked	**¼ cup**	**60 mL**
Quartered pitted dried prunes	**1½ cups**	**375 mL**
Parsley flakes	**½ tsp.**	**2 mL**
Ground thyme	**⅛ tsp.**	**0.5 mL**
Salt	**½ tsp.**	**2 mL**
Pepper	**¼ tsp.**	**1 mL**
Diced cooked chicken	**3 cups**	**750 mL**

Combine first 8 ingredients in large saucepan. Bring to a boil. Cook slowly for about 30 minutes.

Add chicken. Cover. Cook for 10 minutes. Check for salt and pepper, adding more if needed. Makes about 14 cups (3.5 L).

Note: Chicken stock can be made using 10 cups (2.5 L) water plus 3⅓ tbsp. (50 mL) chicken bouillon powder.

Pictured above.

Here are some great recipes that make use of all kinds of rice. Simple and easy to prepare, stove-top recipes generally take less time to cook than meals that are baked in the oven. Enjoy these dishes on their own with a salad and bun, or as a tasty side dish at your next meal.

BROCCOLI RICE STIR-FRY

Prepare wild rice early in the day. Add to the broccoli mixture to heat through. Add an extra dish of white rice, noodles or potatoes if you like, depending on your preference.

Wild rice	¼ cup	60 mL
Water	1 cup	250 mL
Salt	⅛ tsp.	0.5 mL
Broccoli florets and peeled, cut stems	1 cup	250 mL
Small red pepper, cut up	¼	¼
Celery stalk, cut into matchsticks	1	1
Carrot, cut into matchsticks	½	½
Green onion, sliced	1	1
Lemon juice, fresh or bottled	1½ tsp.	7 mL
Cooking oil	2 tsp.	10 mL

Cover rice with water. Swish it around and drain through sieve. Rinse a second time. Cover rice with water and soak for 2 hours. Drain. Put rice, 4 cups (1 L) water and salt into saucepan. Bring to a boil. Simmer, covered, for 50 to 60 minutes until grains burst. Cool.

Put broccoli florets and stems into large wok or frying pan over medium-high heat. Add remaining ingredients along with cooked wild rice. Add only part of the rice if you like the look better. Stir continually for 3 to 5 minutes until vegetables are tender-crisp. Serves 2.

RISOTTO

Prepare rih-SAW-toh when you have extra time. This Italian speciality requires stock to be added in portions while stirring fairly steadily. A creamy rice dish.

Butter or hard margarine	2 tbsp.	30 mL
Finely chopped onion	1 cup	250 mL
Arborio rice (see Note)	1½ cups	375 mL
Instant vegetable stock mix	2 tbsp.	30 mL
Boiling water	5 cups	1.25 L
Red wine (or alcohol-free red wine) or twice as much white wine (optional)	2 tbsp.	30 mL
Grated Parmesan cheese	2 tbsp.	30 mL

Melt butter in heavy saucepan. Add onion. Sauté until soft. Watch that butter doesn't brown.

Add rice. Stir until butter is absorbed without rice getting dry. Be sure to cook slowly.

Stir stock mix into boiling water in separate saucepan. Keep at a simmer. Add 1 cup (250 mL) stock to rice. Stir frequently. When stock is absorbed, add another 1 cup (250 mL) stock. Repeat until all stock has been added. Stir continually until all stock is absorbed. Rice is done when it is creamy, not mushy, and tender but firm. This will take about 25 minutes.

Add wine if using. Stir.

Add cheese. Stir. Remove from heat. Pass extra Parmesan when serving. Makes 4 cups (1 L).

Note: Italian Arborio rice is the kind needed for this recipe. If using Canadian or American short grain rice, you may need to add a little more vegetable stock.

TIP

It is not necessary to salt the water when boiling rice. Salt is only a flavor-enhancer. Substitute 1 tbsp. (15 mL) dried herbs for a slightly different flavor.

Top: Risotto Milanese, page 72
Bottom: Spanish Lentil Pilaf, page 74

RISOTTO MILANESE

This is prepared in a very different way than other rice. A lot of stirring produces a good product. From Northern Italy.

Water	**8 cups**	**2 L**
Chicken bouillon cubes, crushed	**8**	**8**
Saffron, a pinch to make yellow		
Butter or hard margarine	**¹/₂ cup**	**125 mL**
Finely chopped onion	**1 cup**	**250 mL**
Long grain white rice, uncooked	**2 cups**	**500 mL**
Grated Parmesan cheese	**¹/₂ cup**	**125 mL**
Butter or hard margarine	**2 tbsp.**	**30 mL**
Grated Parmesan cheese, heavy sprinkle		

Boil water in large saucepan. Add bouillon cubes. Stir to dissolve. Keep hot.

Measure ¹/₂ cup (125 mL) chicken broth into small saucepan. Add saffron. Stir to dissolve.

Melt first amount of butter in large frying pan. Add onion. Sauté until lightly browned.

Add rice to onion. Stir constantly for 10 to 15 minutes until a light gold color. Add 1 cup (250 mL) chicken broth. Stir until liquid is absorbed. Repeat 3 more times until a total of 4 cups (1 L) chicken broth has been added. Now add saffron-broth mixture. Stir until absorbed.

Add first amount of cheese. Stir. Continue to add chicken broth, 1 cup (250 mL) at a time, until rice is al-denté, tender but firm. Near the end of cooking time add broth in ¹/₂ cup (125 mL) additions. If rice is too dry after all broth has been used, add boiling water in ¹/₄ cup (60 mL) amounts. Total cooking and stirring time is 30 to 35 minutes.

Add second amount of butter. Stir. Transfer to serving bowl. Sprinkle with grated Parmesan cheese. Serves 8.

Pictured on page 71.

JAMBALAYA

A traditional favorite in the southern state of Louisiana. Contains rice, meat and some vegetables.

Cooking oil	3 tbsp.	50 mL
Chicken parts, skin removed	4 lbs.	1.8 kg
Salt, good sprinkle		
Pepper, good sprinkle		
Smoked spicy sausage or smoked ham, cut up	2 lbs.	900 g
Chopped onion	2¹⁄₂ cups	625 mL
Chopped celery	1 cup	250 mL
Chopped green pepper	1 cup	250 mL
Garlic clove, minced	1	1
Boiling water	3 cups	750 mL
Chicken bouillon cubes	3 × ¹⁄₅ oz.	3 × 6 g
Long grain white rice, uncooked	2¹⁄₃ cups	575 mL
Cayenne pepper	¹⁄₄ tsp.	1 mL
Salt	¹⁄₂ tsp.	2 mL

Heat cooking oil in frying pan. Brown chicken. Sprinkle with salt and pepper. Transfer to platter.

Brown sausage, adding more cooking oil if necessary. Transfer to platter.

Combine onion, celery, green pepper and garlic in frying pan. Add more cooking oil if needed. Sauté until tender. Remove from heat.

Put boiling water and bouillon cubes into large pot over medium heat. Stir to dissolve cubes.

Add rice, cayenne pepper and salt to water. Add chicken, sausage and onion mixture. Stir lightly. Cover. Simmer for about 15 minutes to cook rice. Taste for salt, pepper and cayenne. Serves 8.

Pictured on this page and on front cover.

SPANISH LENTIL PILAF

Slightly spicy with a chunky look. Very good.

Canned stewed tomatoes	14 oz.	398 mL
Water	2 cups	500 mL
Brown rice, uncooked	½ cup	125 mL
Green lentils	¼ cup	60 mL
Red lentils	¼ cup	60 mL
Chopped onion	½ cup	125 mL
Chopped celery	¼ cup	60 mL
Instant vegetable stock mix	1 tbsp.	15 mL
Dried sweet basil	1½ tsp.	7 mL
Pepper	¼ tsp.	1 mL
Grated medium or sharp Cheddar cheese	1 cup	250 mL

Measure first 10 ingredients into saucepan. Bring to a boil, stirring often. Simmer, covered, for about 60 minutes until rice and lentils are tender.

Add cheese. Stir until it melts. Makes 3½ cups (875 mL).

Pictured on page 71.

SPANISH RICE

Be sure to try this, especially if you have never tried tomatoes with rice.

Long grain white rice, uncooked	1 cup	250 mL
Condensed onion soup	10 oz.	284 mL
Canned sliced mushrooms, drained (optional)	10 oz.	284 mL
Water	1¼ cups	300 mL
Butter or hard margarine	¼ cup	60 mL
Canned tomatoes, with juice, cut up	1 cup	250 mL

Combine first 5 ingredients in saucepan. Simmer, covered, for about 25 minutes until rice is tender and water is absorbed.

Add tomatoes. Heat through. Serves 4.

TIP

For a new flavor, cook rice in chicken broth (bouillon), beef broth (bouillon) or vegetable stock.

RICE WITH LENTILS

This is a creamy color even though red lentils are added. Contains peas.

Cooking oil	3 tbsp.	50 mL
Whole cardamoms	4	4
Small cinnamon stick, 2 inch (5 cm)	1	1
Whole cloves	4	4
Bay leaves	3	3
Medium onions, sliced	3	3
Basmati rice (or other long grain), uncooked	2¹/₂ cups	625 mL
Split red lentils	¹/₂ cup	125 mL
Peas, fresh or frozen	1 cup	250 mL
Water	6 cups	1.5 L
Salt	1 tbsp.	15 mL
Chicken bouillon powder	1 tbsp.	15 mL

Heat cooking oil in large saucepan. Add next 5 ingredients. Sauté until onion is soft.

Add rice and lentils. Sauté for 3 minutes, stirring often.

Add remaining ingredients. Bring to a boil. Cover. Simmer for about 15 minutes until rice is tender and water is absorbed. Discard bay leaf. Fluff with fork. Serves 8.

Pictured below.

COCONUT RICE CURRY

Good and quite different with the addition of peanuts and browned coconut. Curry is mild.

Long grain white rice	2 cups	500 mL
Chopped onion	¼ cup	60 mL
Water	4 cups	1 L
Salt	1 tsp.	5 mL
Butter or hard margarine	2 tbsp.	30 mL
Unsweetened coconut	¾ cup	175 mL
Salted peanuts, chopped	½ cup	125 mL
Curry powder	1 tsp.	5 mL

Combine rice, onion, water and salt in saucepan. Cook, covered, for about 15 minutes until rice is tender. Water should be absorbed.

Melt butter in frying pan. Add coconut. Sauté until light brown.

Add peanuts and curry powder to coconut. Stir. To serve, mix everything together. An alternate method of serving is to mix half the coconut mixture with rice and sprinkle second half coconut mixture over top. Serves 8.

Pictured on this page.

PERKY RICE

Similar to fried rice without the frying.

Long grain white rice	1½ cups	375 mL
Finely diced carrot	½ cup	125 mL
Finely diced celery	½ cup	125 mL
Finely diced onion	¼ cup	60 mL
Water	3 cups	750 mL
Salt	1 tsp.	5 mL

Place all ingredients in medium heavy saucepan. Cover and bring to a boil. Boil slowly for about 15 minutes until rice is tender and water is absorbed. Leftovers may be frozen. Serves 4.

Measurement Tables

Throughout this book measurements are given in Conventional and Metric measure. To compensate for differences between the two measurements due to rounding, a full metric measure is not always used. The cup used is the standard 8 fluid ounce. Temperature is given in degrees Fahrenheit and Celsius. Baking pan measurements are in inches and centimetres as well as quarts and litres. An exact metric conversion is given below as well as the working equivalent (Standard Measure).

OVEN TEMPERATURES

Fahrenheit (°F)	Celsius (°C)
175°	80°
200°	95°
225°	110°
250°	120°
275°	140°
300°	150°
325°	160°
350°	175°
375°	190°
400°	205°
425°	220°
450°	230°
475°	240°
500°	260°

SPOONS

Conventional Measure	Metric Exact Conversion Millilitre (mL)	Metric Standard Measure Millilitre (mL)
1/8 teaspoon (tsp.)	0.6 mL	0.5 mL
1/4 teaspoon (tsp.)	1.2 mL	1 mL
1/2 teaspoon (tsp.)	2.4 mL	2 mL
1 teaspoon (tsp.)	4.7 mL	5 mL
2 teaspoons (tsp.)	9.4 mL	10 mL
1 tablespoon (tbsp.)	14.2 mL	15 mL

CUPS

1/4 cup (4 tbsp.)	56.8 mL	50 mL
1/3 cup (5 1/3 tbsp.)	75.6 mL	75 mL
1/2 cup (8 tbsp.)	113.7 mL	125 mL
2/3 cup (10 2/3 tbsp.)	151.2 mL	150 mL
3/4 cup (12 tbsp.)	170.5 mL	175 mL
1 cup (16 tbsp.)	227.3 mL	250 mL
4 1/2 cups	1022.9 mL	1000 mL (1 L)

PANS

Conventional Inches	Metric Centimetres
8x8 inch	20x20 cm
9x9 inch	22x22 cm
9x13 inch	22x33 cm
10x15 inch	25x38 cm
11x17 inch	28x43 cm
8x2 inch round	20x5 cm
9x2 inch round	22x5 cm
10x4 1/2 inch tube	25x11 cm
8x4x3 inch loaf	20x10x7 cm
9x5x3 inch loaf	22x12x7 cm

DRY MEASUREMENTS

Conventional Measure Ounces (oz.)	Metric Exact Conversion Grams (g)	Metric Standard Measure Grams (g)
1 oz.	28.3 g	30 g
2 oz.	56.7 g	55 g
3 oz.	85.0 g	85 g
4 oz.	113.4 g	125 g
5 oz.	141.7 g	140 g
6 oz.	170.1 g	170 g
7 oz.	198.4 g	200 g
8 oz.	226.8 g	250 g
16 oz.	453.6 g	500 g
32 oz.	907.2 g	1000 g (1 kg)

CASSEROLES (CANADA & BRITAIN)

Standard Size Casserole	Exact Metric Measure
1 qt. (5 cups)	1.13 L
1 1/2 qts. (7 1/2 cups)	1.69 L
2 qts. (10 cups)	2.25 L
2 1/2 qts. (12 1/2 cups)	2.81 L
3 qts. (15 cups)	3.38 L
4 qts. (20 cups)	4.5 L
5 qts. (25 cups)	5.63 L

CASSEROLES (UNITED STATES)

Standard Size Casserole	Exact Metric Measure
1 qt. (4 cups)	900 mL
1 1/2 qts. (6 cups)	1.35 L
2 qts. (8 cups)	1.8 L
2 1/2 qts. (10 cups)	2.25 L
3 qts. (12 cups)	2.7 L
4 qts. (16 cups)	3.6 L
5 qts. (20 cups)	4.5 L

Index

RICE

COOKBOOKS

Risotto Milanese, page 72

Creating everyday recipes you can trust!

Company's Coming cookbooks are available at retail locations everywhere.

For information contact:

COMPANY'S COMING PUBLISHING LIMITED

Box 8037, Station "F"
Edmonton, Alberta
Canada T6H 4N9

Box 17870
San Diego, California
U.S.A. 92177-7870

TEL: (403) 450-6223
FAX: (403) 450-1857